DISCOVER AMERICA

OREGON

Jay D. Winans

AV² provides enriched content that supplements and complements this book. Weigl's AV² books strive to create inspired learning and engage young minds in a total learning experience.

Your AV² Media Enhanced books come alive with...

Audio
Listen to sections of the book read aloud.

Key Words
Study vocabulary, and complete a matching word activity.

Video
Watch informative video clips.

Quizzes
Test your knowledge.

Embedded Weblinks
Gain additional information for research.

Slide Show
View images and captions, and prepare a presentation.

Try This!
Complete activities and hands-on experiments.

Go to **www.av2books.com**, and enter this book's unique code.

BOOK CODE

N 5 6 9 3 4 8

AV² by Weigl brings you media enhanced books that support active learning.

... and much, much more!

Published by AV² by Weigl
350 5th Avenue, 59th Floor
New York, NY 10118
Website: www.av2books.com

Library of Congress Cataloging-in-Publication Data
Names: Winans, Jay D., author.
Title: Oregon : the Beaver State / Jay D. Winans.
Description: New York, NY : AV2 by Weigl, [2016] | Series: Discover America |
  Includes index.
Identifiers: LCCN 2015048035 (print) | LCCN 2015048334 (ebook) | ISBN
  9781489649263 (hard cover : alk. paper) | ISBN 9781489649270 (soft cover :
  alk. paper) | ISBN 9781489649287 (Multi-User eBook)
Subjects: LCSH: Oregon--Juvenile literature.
Classification: LCC F876.3 .W563 2016 (print) | LCC F876.3 (ebook) | DDC 979.5--dc23
LC record available at http://lccn.loc.gov/2015048035

Printed in the United States of America, in Brainerd, Minnesota
1 2 3 4 5 6 7 8 9 20 19 18 17 16

052016
270516

Project Coordinator Heather Kissock
Art Director Terry Paulhus

Photo Credits
Every reasonable effort has been made to trace ownership and to obtain permission to reprint copyright material. The publisher would be pleased to have any errors or omissions brought to their attention so that they may be corrected in subsequent printings. The publisher acknowledges Getty Images, iStock Images, Newscom, and Alamy as its primary image suppliers for this title.

OREGON

Contents

STATE TREE
Douglas Fir

STATE BIRD
Western Meadowlark

STATE OF OREGON

1859

STATE FLAG
Oregon

STATE FRUIT
Pear

STATE FLOWER
Oregon Grape

STATE SEAL
Oregon

Nickname
The Beaver State

Motto
She Flies With Her
Own Wings

Song
"Oregon, My Oregon," words
by J. A. Buchanan and music
by Henry B. Murtagh

Population
(2014 Census) 3,970,239
Ranked 27th state

Entered the Union
February 14, 1859, as the 33rd State

Capital
Salem

Discover Oregon

Located in a region of the United States called the Pacific Northwest, Oregon has attracted visitors for centuries. Today, Oregon's stunning combination of mountains, forest, and coastline has led many to refer to the state as the Pacific Wonderland. The state is known for its forestry and fishing industries. During the second half of the twentieth century, these industries were threatened.

Overfishing of salmon and extensive logging in forests led to a severe decline of these resources. The northern spotted owl nearly became **extinct** when its habitat was threatened by logging. Environmental protection laws were created to protect the state's natural resources. While Oregon's traditional industries were forced to adapt to these challenges, new high-technology industries, such as electronics, developed and strengthened the state's economy.

Oregon is a haven for outdoor recreation. The mountains and coastline provide a wealth of opportunity for activities such as swimming, skiing, boating, hiking, hunting, and fishing. The Columbia River Gorge in northern Oregon has become one of the most popular places in the world to windsurf. Oregon's friendly population and diversified economy attract people from all over the world.

Oregon's road network is extensive. Running the length of the Oregon coast, the Pacific Coast Scenic Byway offers spectacular views of the picturesque coastline. Portland International Airport is the largest airport in Oregon. The airline industry is an important part of Oregon's economy as Portland and other airports serve as gateways to Asia.

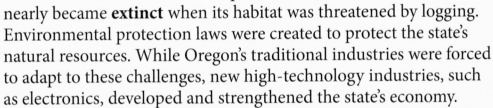

The Land

Oregon is **nicknamed** the **Beaver State**. Beaver fur was an **important source** of income for early trappers and fur traders in Oregon.

Many modern place names in Oregon are based on words from the Chinook Native Americans. These include **Clackmas, Multnomah, Wasco, Cathlamet, and Clatsop.**

Cannon Beach was named for the cannon from the shipwrecked *USS Shark* that washed ashore in 1846. In 2013, *National Geographic* magazine named Cannon Beach one of the world's 100 Most Beautiful Places.

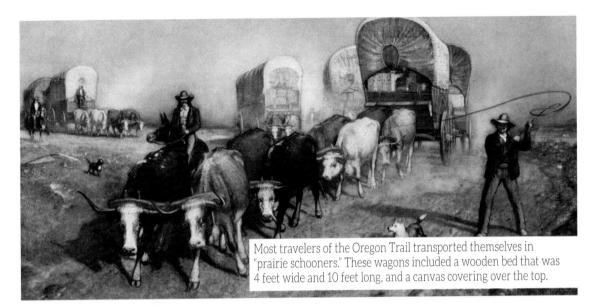

Most travelers of the Oregon Trail transported themselves in "prairie schooners." These wagons included a wooden bed that was 4 feet wide and 10 feet long, and a canvas covering over the top.

Beginnings

Spanish explorers may have first sailed the coastal waters of Oregon as early as 1543. Eventually, many European nations were drawn to the area for its wealth of fur-bearing animals and their valuable pelts. Following the **Louisiana Purchase** of 1803, U.S. President Thomas Jefferson sent Meriwether Lewis and William Clark to explore the North American continent west of the Mississippi River. Their successful **expedition** to the Oregon coast encouraged fur trappers and traders and then settlers to journey to Oregon throughout the 1800s.

In the mid-1800s, some 300,000 to 500,000 pioneers followed the Oregon Trail westward from Missouri. Many of them continued all the way to Oregon's fertile Willamette Valley. These early settlers were attracted to the state's abundant supply of furs, its fertile land, and its rich forests. Their journey has been called the Great **Migration**.

With the European settlers came European diseases, which resulted in the deaths of many Native Americans. Competition between the settlers and the Native Americans over valuable land and natural resources often developed into violent conflicts. In 1823, the U.S. Supreme Court ruled that because the Native Americans were "wanderers," they did not own their land. In 1859, Oregon became the 33rd state of the United States. Logging and farming industries fueled the new economy.

Where is OREGON?

Oregon's western border follows the Pacific coast. The state is bordered by Washington to the north, Idaho to the east, and California and Nevada to the south. The Columbia River forms most of the border, dividing Oregon from Washington. The Snake River forms a large section of the border dividing Oregon from Idaho.

3

4

Portland

☆ **Salem**

1

Pacific Ocean

United States Map

← Oregon

Alaska Hawai'i

MAP LEGEND

■ Oregon
☆ Capital City
● Major City
〰 Columbia River
▲ Tillamook State Forest
□ Bordering States
□ Water

---

1 Salem

Salem is Oregon's state capital. The site was first settled in 1840 by **missionaries** and quickly grew. It has been the state capital since 1855. Today, more than 161,000 people call Salem home. In the summer, visitors and residents can enjoy a variety of outdoor festivals. Several museums and city parks are also available.

2 Columbia River

The Columbia River winds its way along the northern border of the state. Running more than 2,000 miles in total, it is the largest U.S. river to flow into the Pacific Ocean. The Columbia River serves as a strong source of hydroelectric power for the United States.

WASHINGTON

Columbia River

2

OREGON

IDAHO

N

SCALE 0 ——— 50 miles

3 Portland

Located about 43 miles northeast of Salem is the city of Portland. The state's largest city, Portland has a population of more than 600,000. Many of these people work in the technology industry, Portland's strongest industrial sector.

4 Tillamook State Forest

Nestled in the state's Coast Range, Tillamook State Forest is a popular recreational area for the state. The forest covers approximately 364,000 acres and is home to a wide variety of animal and plant species.

Land Features

Oregon has a varied landscape, which stretches from the Pacific Ocean to the Blue Mountains in the northeast. The western third of the state is mountainous and lush with dense rainforests. Between the state's coastal mountains and the higher Cascade Mountains farther inland is the Willamette Valley. The valley's fertile soil is good for growing many kinds of agricultural products. East of the Cascade Mountains, the eastern part of Oregon is a dry region of open plains and deserts. Oregon's coastline is made up largely of steep cliffs. The Columbia is Oregon's major river, and its main tributary is the Snake River.

Multnomah Falls

The highest waterfall in Oregon is Multnomah Falls, which is located on the south side of the Columbia River Gorge.

Mount Hood

The highest point in the state is Mount Hood. Located in the Cascade Mountains, it rises 11,239 feet above sea level.

Crater Lake

At 1,932 feet deep, Crater Lake is the deepest lake in the United States and the seventh-deepest lake in the world.

Hells Canyon

Parts of Hells Canyon, on the Oregon-Idaho border, are nearly 8,000 feet deep. At the bottom of the canyon is the Snake River.

Climate

Oregon's coastal regions enjoy a mild climate, with January temperatures ranging from freezing to about 45° Fahrenheit. In July, coastal temperatures average about 65°F. Very wet winters allow for the lush, green forests of the region.

The interior also tends to have colder winters, and January's average temperature in the east can dip to as low as 25°F. The Cascade region receives large amounts of snowfall, commonly beginning in October and lasting until April, although some snowfields last through July.

Average Annual Precipitation Across Oregon

Many people think that the entire state of Oregon receives a large amount of rain, but some cities are actually quite dry. Why might some parts of the state receive much more precipitation than others?

LEGEND

Average Annual Precipitation (in inches) 1961–1990

200 – 100.1

100 – 25.1

25 – 5 and less

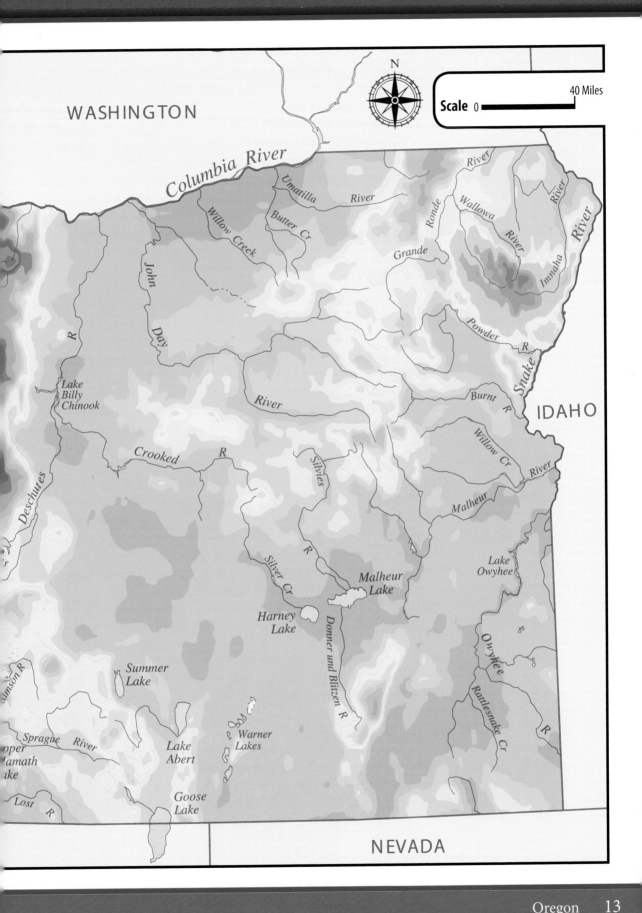

WASHINGTON

Columbia River

N

River

Umatilla *River*

Butter Cr

Ronde

Wallowa *River*

Innaha *River*

Snake River

Willow Creek

Grande

John Day

Powder R

R

Lake
Billy
Chinook

River

Burnt R

IDAHO

Crooked *R*

Willow Cr

River

Deschutes

Silvies

Malheur

R

Silver Cr

Malheur
Lake

Lake
Owyhee

Harney
Lake

Donner und Blitzen R

Owyhee

inson R

Summer
Lake

Rattlesnake Cr

R

Sprague *River*

Lake
Abert

Warner
Lakes

oper
lamath
ke

Lost *R*

Goose
Lake

NEVADA

Oregon 13

Nature's Resources

One of Oregon's greatest resources is its high-quality Jory soil, which is named after an early pioneer family. More than 300,000 acres of Jory soil can be found in the rolling hills around the Willamette Valley. The deep, well-drained soil is excellent for agriculture and forestry.

Forests are found throughout the state. In fact, nearly half of Oregon is covered with forests. West of the Cascades, most of the trees are Douglas firs. Ponderosa pines are the most common trees east of the Cascades. The abundant forests provided the raw materials for logging, Oregon's first major industry.

Much of Oregon's cattle is raised in the eastern half of the state, where the soil is too poor to grow crops.

Much of Oregon is mountainous. The eastern part of the state and the wide valleys between the mountain ranges provide excellent grasslands. The land is used for farming wheat, barley, and vegetables, and also for cattle grazing. Cattle is Oregon's most important livestock. Its most important agricultural product is wheat.

The Willamette Valley's good soil supports many crops, including grapes.

In the 1980s, logging in Oregon was reduced on federally owned land in an effort to preserve old growth forests.

Vegetation

Oregon's landscape is a spectacular combination of forests and vibrant wildflowers. Cedars, cottonwoods, firs, maples, pines, and spruces all grow in Oregon's forests. The state tree is the Douglas fir, which was named after David Douglas, a Scottish botanist who visited the area in 1825. These giant trees average 200 feet in height with a trunk diameter of 6 feet. They can grow as tall as 325 feet, with a 15-foot trunk diameter. The Douglas fir has contributed significantly to Oregon's extensive logging industry.

Columbia Lily

The Columbia lily grows well in mountainous regions, at elevations of 6,000 feet. It is also known as the tiger lily.

Blackberry Bushes

Wild blackberry bushes are common throughout the state. Many gardeners consider them pests because the bushes grow quickly and are hard to get rid of.

Oregon Grape

The berries of this plant are not actually grapes, but they are edible when ripe. The Oregon grape is commonly found along the Pacific coast.

Horsetail Fern

Horsetail ferns grow well in Oregon's damp soil. The plant gets its name from the spines along its top, which look similar to a horse's tail.

Wildlife

Oregon has a thriving animal population. The state is home to a variety of large animals, including black bears, bighorn sheep, elk, mule deer, pronghorn antelope, and white-tailed deer. Smaller animals are even more numerous. Bobcats, gray and red foxes, martens, muskrats, minks, raccoons, otters, badgers, coyotes, opossums, beavers, and skunks can all be found in Oregon.

Oregon's coastal waters are home to sea otters and sea lions. Once numerous, salmon, halibut, and other species of fish are now carefully monitored to protect their numbers. The bull trout has been identified by the U.S. Fish and Wildlife Service as a threatened species in the Columbia River.

Northern Spotted Owl

The northern spotted owl is listed as a threatened species in Oregon, Washington, and California. The owl makes its home in old-growth forests, which have been largely destroyed by the logging industry.

Beaver

Oregon's state animal was once almost wiped out by fur trappers. Today, beavers are protected by state law and can be found building dams in rivers throughout the state.

Great Blue Heron

The wingspan of the great blue heron can be as wide as 6 feet. The birds can be found along Oregon's Pacific shoreline or on the banks of its larger rivers.

Chinook Salmon

The Chinook salmon is the largest type of Pacific salmon. Also known as the spring, king, or tyee salmon, it is Oregon's state fish.

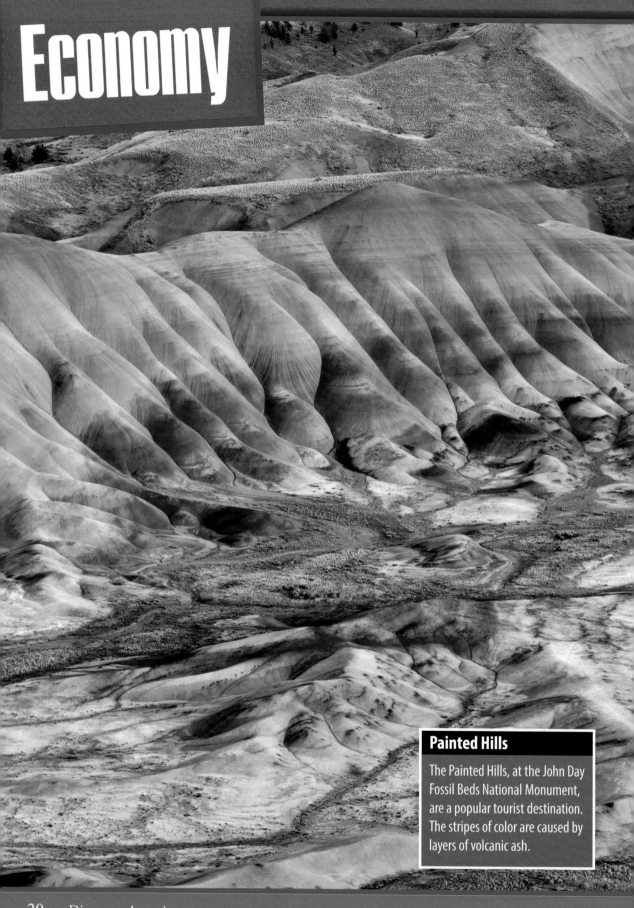

Economy

Painted Hills

The Painted Hills, at the John Day Fossil Beds National Monument, are a popular tourist destination. The stripes of color are caused by layers of volcanic ash.

Tourism

The coastline, mountain ranges, canyons, volcanoes, and forests of Oregon offer abundant recreational opportunities and attract tourists to the state. Oregonians are careful to balance tourism and environmental protection. The state has more than 300 miles of protected natural coastline, most of which can be enjoyed by driving along the Pacific Coast Scenic Byway. The route provides travelers with views of beautiful rugged coastline and white sand dunes.

Mountain climbers, rock climbers, and hikers from around the world are drawn to Oregon's numerous mountain ranges. Mount Hood is a popular destination for mountaineers. Mount Ashland and other peaks of the Klamath Mountains offer pristine hiking opportunities.

Oregon Zoo

The Oregon Zoo, in Portland, has been in operation since 1887. More than 1 million people visit the zoo every year.

Heceta Head Lighthouse

Heceta Head Lighthouse, on the southern part of Oregon's Pacific coast, was first lit in 1894, and it is still a working lighthouse today. It is rumored that the lighthouse is haunted by the ghost of a woman named Rue.

Oregon Coast Aquarium

Located in Newport, the Oregon Coast Aquarium was once home to Keiko, the orca who starred in the *Free Willy* movies. Exhibits at the aquarium feature many types of sea life, including otters and seals.

As of 2013, Oregon's forestry industry employs about 76,000 people. Forestry in Oregon generates $12.7 billion in profit each year.

Primary Industries

Manufacturing is an important part of Oregon's economy. The production of forest products such as lumber, plywood, pulp, and paper remains a major industry. Although the industry's importance began to decline in the 1980s, the state is still the largest lumber producer in the country. To protect animal habitats and the rainforests, tree harvesting in Oregon is done in an environmentally sensitive manner.

In the 1990s, mostly due to the decline in the forest-products industry, high technology became an increasingly important part of Oregon's economy. High-tech industries include the manufacture of electronics and electrical products, computer software, computer equipment, and semiconductors.

More than **1,700 people** are employed in Oregon's commercial fishing industry.

More than **15 million passengers** traveled through Portland International Airport in **2013**.

Value of Goods and Services (in Millions of Dollars)

Many workers in Oregon are employed in industries that provide services to people. Stores, hotels, restaurants, and health care facilities are all part of service industries. What are some of the kinds of services that people in the health care industry provide?

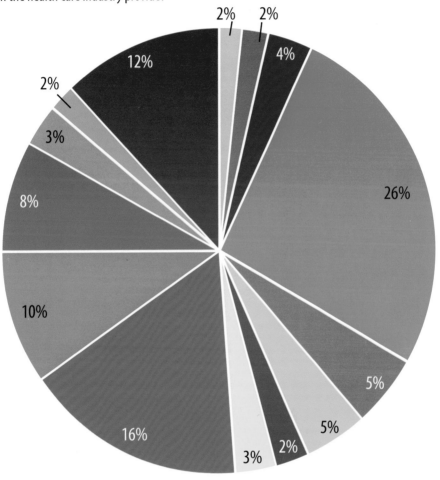

⬤ Agriculture, Forestry, and Fishing		$4,055
Mining		$331*
⬤ Utilities		$3,684
⬤ Construction		$7,506
⬤ Manufacturing		$55,961
⬤ Wholesale Trade		$11,104
⬤ Retail Trade		$9,971
⬤ Transportation and Warehousing		$5,247

⬤ Information		$6,561
⬤ Finance, Insurance, and Real Estate		$34,919
⬤ Professional and Business Services		$20,821
⬤ Education, Health and Social Services		$17,007
⬤ Recreation and Accommodations		$6,589
⬤ Other Services		$4,131
⬤ Government		$24,920

*less than 1%

Goods and Services

Oregon, which has more than 40,000 farms, is well known for the diversity of its agriculture. The state's different climate zones and rich soils produce a wide variety of crops. Christmas trees, hazelnuts, peppermint, green beans, cherries, and onions are all grown in Oregon.

The Willamette Valley is an exceptional location to grow specialty fruits such as berries and cherries.

Commercial fishing is an important part of Oregon's economy. Shellfish such as oysters, mussels, clams, shrimp, crabs, and scallops are harvested on the coast. Although overfishing has led to a decline in Oregon's salmon fishing industry, salmon is still an important commercial catch.

Oregon's commercial fishing industry brought more than $148 million to the state in 2011.

The service sector plays a dominant role in Oregon's economy, accounting for about three-fourths of the jobs in the state. Wholesale and retail firms are among the state's largest employers. Other important service industries include banking, government, real estate, and health and social services.

Pendleton, Oregon, is known for Pendleton wool. Pendleton mill was originally founded in 1893, and was then expanded in 1909 to include a retail space.

Chief Joseph was a leader of the Nez Percé. He was born Hinmuuttu-yalatlat, which means "Thunder rolling down the mountain."

Native Americans

Long before settlers of European descent arrived, as many as 180,000 Native Americans lived in the Oregon region. When the explorers Lewis and Clark arrived in the Oregon area in 1805, they noted in their journals that Oregon was populated by many thousands of Native Americans. The Native Americans who lived in what is now Oregon before the arrival of the settlers belonged to about 125 tribes. Among them were the Chinook, the Nez Percé, the Umatilla, the Paiute, and Klamath and Modoc.

Contact with these new settlers caused many Native American groups living in the area to be wiped out by disease after only a few decades. The Native Americans had no natural defenses against the diseases brought by the newcomers, which included malaria, chickenpox, measles, and whooping cough. A long series of wars, lasting from 1847 to 1880, also took its toll on the Native American population. By the 1880s, most of the state's remaining Native Americans had been forced onto **reservations**.

Traditional clothing of the Umatilla Native Americans included deer, elk, and buffalo hide. Moccasins and fringe decorations were also common.

Exploring the Land

The area that became Oregon attracted the interest of many different European nations. The Spanish explorer Bartolomé Ferrelo, seeking the **Northwest Passage** as part of an expedition led by João Rodrigues Cabrilho, may have sailed the Oregon coastline as early as 1543. Some historians believe that the British explorer Sir Francis Drake sailed along Oregon's coast in 1579, but there is little evidence to support this.

Timeline of Settlement

Further Exploration and Settlement

1775 Spanish explorer Bruno de Hezeta is the first European to find the mouth of the Columbia River. His name is sometimes spelled Heceta.

1774 Spanish Explorer Juan José Pérez maps the coast of the Pacific Northwest.

1792 Captain Robert Gray becomes the first person of European descent to sail into the mouth of the Columbia River.

1543 Spanish navigator Bartolomé Ferrelo becomes the first European explorer to see the Oregon coast.

1811 John Jacob Astor sets up a trading settlement at the mouth of the Columbia River.

Early Exploration

1834 A missionary named Jason Lee establishes a school for Native Americans in Salem.

Another Spanish seafarer, Sebastian Vizcaino, may have sighted Oregon in 1603 and named Cape Sebastian, north of the California border. By the 1700s, Russians had begun exploring the area in search of an abundant source of furs. The British were also interested in the Pacific Northwest. Two British companies, the Hudson's Bay Company and the North West Company, sent men to explore the area and expand the fur trade.

In 1792, Captain Robert Gray, a trader from the United States, became the first person of European descent to sail into the mouth of the Columbia River. He named the river after his ship, the *Columbia Rediviva*. The United States soon claimed the Pacific Northwest based on Gray's exploration of the river.

1848 The U.S. Congress establishes the Oregon Territory.

Gold and Statehood

1851 Gold is discovered in Oregon.

1843 Pioneers begin traveling in large numbers to the Oregon Country along the Oregon Trail.

Oregon Trail

1859 President James Buchanan signs documents making Oregon a state on February 14th.

Sacajawea played an important role in Lewis and Clark's expedition, acting as an interpreter and diplomat during their encounters with Native American groups.

The First Settlers

Under the terms of the Louisiana Purchase, the United States acquired a vast amount of territory from France, extending from the Mississippi River to the Rocky Mountains. In May 1804, Meriwether Lewis and William Clark left St. Louis, Missouri, to lead an expedition to explore this land and continue west all the way to the Pacific Ocean. They traveled up the Missouri River until they reached the Rockies. They continued by land through the mountains, and then traveled down the Snake and Columbia Rivers.

In the winter of 1804 to 1805, Lewis and Clark hired the **interpreters** Toussaint Charbonneau and his wife, Sacagawea. Sacagawea, who was a Shoshone, was an important addition to Lewis and Clark's party. She was able to guide them through the land of the Shoshone. She also helped them find edible fruits and vegetables to supplement their diet.

The expedition nearly ended in the late summer of 1805 when it met bad weather in the Rocky Mountains and ran out of provisions. The party was saved by Nez Percé Native Americans, who fed the explorers and helped them on their way through the Rockies. Lewis and Clark established a camp, Fort Clatsop, during the winter of 1805 to 1806 at the site of what is now Seaside, Oregon. They returned to St. Louis in September 1806.

An 1846 **treaty** with Great Britain established the Oregon Country as part of the United States, with the northern boundary at the 49th parallel. Today, that parallel is the northern border of Washington State. It forms part of the border between Canada and the United States.

In 1848, the U.S. government defined the Oregon Territory as the area from the **Continental Divide** to the coast and from the 49th parallel to the 42nd parallel. The Oregon Territory's boundaries did not last long. In 1853, an influx of settlers north of the Columbia River prompted the creation of the Washington Territory. When Oregon became a state in 1859, its present, nearly rectangular boundary was established.

At the turn of the twentieth century, more than two-thirds of Oregonians lived in rural farming communities.

History Makers

Many notable Oregonians contributed to the development of their state and country. The state's well-known residents include Native American leaders, Nobel Prize winners, business entrepreneurs, and environmental activists. Notable Oregonians even include a president of the United States.

Chief Joseph (c. 1840–1904)

Chief Joseph, a leader of the Nez Percé, was born around 1840 in northeastern Oregon. After violence broke out between Caucasian settlers and his people, Chief Joseph tried to lead the Nez Percé to safety in Canada. Chased by the U.S. Cavalry, he and his people avoided capture for months, until he was finally forced to surrender. The Nez Percé were taken to a reservation in what is now Oklahoma and later relocated to a reservation in Washington State.

Herbert Hoover (1874–1964)

Herbert Hoover was born in Iowa but grew up in Newberg, Oregon. He attended Stanford University and became a successful mining engineer. He was elected U.S. president in 1928 and served one term, during which the stock market crashed. This event plunged the United States into the Great Depression, a time of severe economic hardship. During his term, Hoover signed an act naming "The Star-Spangled Banner" as the official anthem of the United States.

Linus Pauling (1901–1994)

Linus Pauling was born in Portland and graduated from Oregon State College in 1922. He also received a Ph.D. in chemistry from the California Institute of Technology. Pauling published hundreds of scientific research papers in his lifetime and was awarded a Nobel Prize for Chemistry in 1954. In 1962, he won the Nobel Peace Prize for his anti-war efforts. He is the only person to win two unshared Nobel Prizes in two different fields.

Mark Hatfield (1922–2011)

Born in Dallas, Oregon, Mark Hatfield served for 30 years as a United States senator. He was also chairman of the Senate Appropriations Committee. In 1993, he became the longest-serving U.S. senator from Oregon. After retiring from office, he became a professor at George Fox University in Newberg.

Phil Knight (1938–)

Born in Portland, Phil Knight attended the University of Oregon in Eugene, where he ran track under coach Bill Bowerman. Knight and Bowerman started a footwear distribution company in 1964. That company became Nike, now a leading global sportswear and athletic supply firm.

Culture

Much of eastern Oregon is desolate compared to the fertile land west of the Cascade Mountains. The land is used for ranching and is still considered a frontier.

Roughly 60 percent of Oregon's population lives in the Portland metropolitan area.

The People Today

More than 3.8 million people live in Oregon. Portland is Oregon's most populous city, followed by Salem and Eugene. The vast majority of the state's residents live west of the Cascade Mountains.

Oregon has been experiencing a population boom. In the 1990s, the population of Oregon increased by more than 20 percent. The population of the United States as a whole increased by 13 percent. From 2000 to 2010, Oregon's population grew by another 12 percent, which was higher than the national average of less than 10 percent. People in Oregon still have plenty of living space. The average number of people per square mile in the nation is a little more than 87, but in Oregon the average is about 40 people per square mile.

Oregon's population **increased** by **more than 400,000** people from **2000 to 2010.**

Q What are some of the reasons that many people from other states and other countries are choosing to move to Oregon?

The Oregon capitol building was placed on the National Register of Historic Places in 1988.

State Government

The governor of Oregon serves as head of the executive branch of government and is elected to a four-year term. The legislature has two chambers, or parts. There is a 60-member House of Representatives, whose members serve two-year terms. The Senate has 30 members, who serve four-year terms. The highest court in Oregon is the Supreme Court, which is made up of seven elected justices who serve six-year terms. Oregon's judicial system has municipal, justice, district, and county courts as well as a court of appeals.

Cities and counties in Oregon can form their own government under a system called home rule. Most have chosen the council form of government headed by either a mayor or city manager. Only 7 of Oregon's 36 counties presently have their own system of government.

The floor of Oregon's House chamber is covered by custom carpet. The pattern includes a Douglas Fir, representing the importance of forestry to the state.

Oregon's governor Kate Brown is the state's second female governor.

Oregon's state song is called **"Oregon, My Oregon."**

Land of the Empire Builders,
Land of the Golden West;

Conquered and held by free men,
Fairest and the best.

On-ward and upward ever,
Forward and on, and on;

Hail to thee, Land of the
Heroes, My Oregon.

Land of the rose and sunshine,
Land of the summer's breeze;

Laden with health and vigor,
Fresh from the western seas.

Blest by the blood of martyrs,
Land of the setting sun;

Hail to thee, Land of Promise,
My Oregon.

* excerpted

Eugene's Oregon Asian Festival celebrates Asian culture from around the world, including China, Japan, Korea, and Vietnam.

Celebrating Culture

Junction City pays homage each year to the cultures of Denmark, Finland, Norway, and Sweden, with the Scandinavian Festival. Entertainment, activities, and displays of Old World crafts are part of the celebration. During the four-day festival in August, downtown Junction City is transformed into an old-fashioned Scandinavian town. Popular events include folk dancing and storytelling.

The Oregon Asian Festival is held in Eugene every February. At this event, traditional Asian cultures are celebrated with demonstrations of martial arts, dance performances, and artwork exhibitions. The festival is one of the largest volunteer-driven events on the West Coast.

The Polish Festival in Portland began as an annual dinner at St. Stanislaus Church. The event has grown to become a large celebration of Polish culture. Thousands of people attend the two-day event, which features stage performances, dance groups, a **polka** contest, street dancing, and Polish cuisine.

Oregon's agricultural heritage is celebrated at events such as Sutherlin's Annual Blackberry Festival. This festival features blackberry cook-offs, craft and food booths, mud volleyball, and lawn mower races. It also raises money to provide local students with college scholarships.

The Flock and Fiber Festival, in Canby, celebrates the region's sheep-raising and wool-processing industries. The three-day festival features a sheep show, with top sheep winning prizes in different categories. Wool garments and crafts are on display throughout the festival.

Chief Joseph Days is held in the city of Joseph, Oregon. This festival celebrates the life of Chief Joseph, his Nez Percé tribe, and the cowboy culture of Oregon's early settlement.

Portland's Cinco de Mayo Fiesta features mariachi music and traditional dance performances.

The Oregon Shakespeare Festival boasts three stages where plays are performed. The Allen Elizabethan Theatre, where the 2014 production of *Into the Woods* was staged, is an outdoor stage and a replica of Shakespeare's Globe theater.

Arts and Entertainment

Cultural and artistic life in Oregon is centered around the state's largest cities and fine educational institutions, such as Oregon State University at Corvallis and the University of Oregon at Eugene. Symphony orchestras, ballet and modern dance companies, choirs, and theatrical companies are found in Portland, Eugene, and Salem. Some major annual entertainment events have contributed to Oregon's reputation in the arts. Perhaps the best known is the Oregon Shakespeare Festival in Ashland. Founded in 1935, the festival now features one of the most respected Shakespearean troupes in the country. Every year, from February through October, the company performs a selection of plays by Shakespeare and other renowned playwrights.

Matt Groening, creator of **The Simpsons**, was born in Portland. In 2009, the show surpassed Gunsmoke as the **longest-running prime-time entertainment series** in the United States.

A Portland band called the **Kingsmen** had a **huge hit** with the rock-and-roll classic "**Louie Louie**" in the mid-1960s.

The Oregon Coast Music Festival was founded in 1979. It is a three-day festival that celebrates the music of the classical composer Joseph Haydn. Since then, it has grown into a two-week celebration of everything from classical music to jazz, bluegrass, and world music.

Many celebrated authors have come from Oregon. John Reed, the author of *Ten Days That Shook the World*, was born in Portland in 1887. Ken Kesey, the author of *One Flew over the Cuckoo's Nest*, was raised in Oregon. Raymond Carver was the author of numerous short stories and collections of poetry. He was born in Clatskanie in 1938. His short stories have been praised as some of the best **literature** from the United States in the late twentieth century.

Author John Reed grew up in Portland, Oregon. He went on to attend Harvard University for Journalism. His life story was made into an Academy Award-winning movie, *Reds*.

Oregon's Pickathon Music Festival is an annual celebration of music. It has hosted such notable performers as blues singer and guitarist Little Freddie King.

Sports and Recreation

Basketball fans in Oregon follow the Portland Trail Blazers. This National Basketball Association (NBA) team was formed in 1970. In just seven years, the team went from being one of the worst teams in basketball to being one of the best. The Trail Blazers won the NBA Finals in 1977, creating the phenomenon Oregonians know as "Blazermania." Since then, the team has continued to attract large, enthusiastic crowds, first at Memorial Coliseum and then, after 1995, at the Rose Garden. The Trail Blazers were Oregon's only major professional sports team until 2011, when the Portland Timbers became a Major League Soccer team.

From 1977 to 1995, the Portland Trailblazers sold out 814 straight home games, one of the longest streaks in U.S. professional sports history.

Dave Kingman, a Major League Baseball player born in Pendleton, hit **442 home runs** during his professional career in the 1970s and 1980s.

Steve Prefontaine was a gifted distance runner whose life was cut short by a car accident at the age of 24. He is **honored every year** with a **memorial run** in his hometown of Coos Bay.

In addition to the Blazers and Timbers, many Oregonians enjoy watching minor league teams. The Portland Winterhawks are Oregon's Western Hockey League team. Minor league baseball has had a home in Oregon since the turn of the 20th century, and fans root for the Eugene Emeralds and the Salem-Keizer Volcanoes.

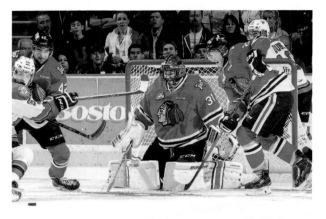

The Portland Winterhawks were founded in 1951. The team was the Western Hockey League Champion in 2013.

College and university teams enjoy loyal followings as well. The University of Oregon Ducks, the Oregon State Beavers, the Pacific University Boxers, and the Willamette University Bearcats are all outstanding entertainment. Autzen Stadium, home of the Ducks and their dedicated fans, is known to be one of the loudest stadiums in all of college football.

The Oregon Ducks have quickly become one of the National Collegiate Athletic Association's (NCAA) more popular football teams. Many Ducks have gone on to play in the NFL, including former Ducks quarterback Marcus Mariota.

Get To Know
OREGON

According to Oregon law, canned corn is not to be used as bait for fishing.

Oregon has **more ghost towns** than any other U.S. state.

AT **121 FEET** IN LENGTH, OREGON'S D RIVER IS THE **SHORTEST RIVER** IN THE WORLD.

THE STATE'S BIRTHDAY IS ON VALENTINE'S DAY.

Oregon is home to **25%** of the country's **llama** population.

99% of the United States' **hazelnut crop** is grown in Oregon.

FUEL OIL

There are **no** **self-serve gas stations** in Oregon.

Brain Teasers

What have you learned about Oregon after reading this book? Test your knowledge by answering these questions. All of the information can be found in the text you just read. The answers are provided below for easy reference.

1 What is the capital of Oregon?

2 What land form falls between the Coast Range and the Cascade Range?

3 Who was the first European to see the Oregon coast?

4 What was the name of the woman who helped to guide explorers Lewis and Clark through Shoshone land?

5 In what year did Oregon become a state?

6 Who serves as the head of the Oregon government's executive branch?

7 Which Oregonian wrote *One Flew Over the Cuckoo's Nest*?

8 Which Oregon river is the shortest in the world?

Key Words

Continental Divide: an imaginary line along the Rocky Mountains that separates those rivers that flow west to the Pacific Ocean and those that flow east to the Atlantic Ocean

expedition: a long journey, usually to explore

extinct: died out

interpreters: people who translate speech from one language to another

literature: books and writings

Louisiana Purchase: a large amount of territory west of the Mississippi River purchased from France by the United States in 1803

migration: a movement of people from one place to another

missionaries: people sent to another country to do charitable work and convert others to their religion

Northwest Passage: an ice-free waterway from the Atlantic Ocean to the Pacific Ocean that was thought to exist

polka: a dance of Bohemian origin

reservations: areas of land set aside for occupation by Native Americans

treaty: formal agreement

Index

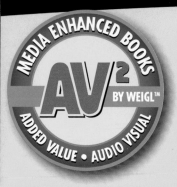

Log on to www.av2books.com

AV² by Weigl brings you media enhanced books that support active learning. Go to www.av2books.com, and enter the special code found on page 2 of this book. You will gain access to enriched and enhanced content that supplements and complements this book. Content includes video, audio, weblinks, quizzes, a slide show, and activities.

AV² Online Navigation

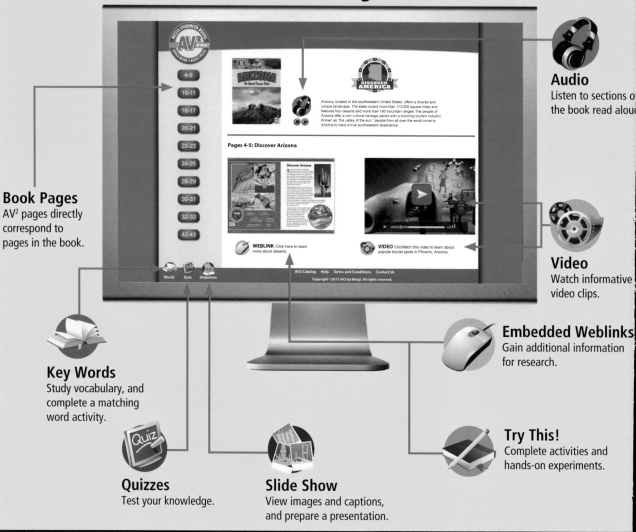

Book Pages
AV² pages directly correspond to pages in the book.

Audio
Listen to sections of the book read aloud

Video
Watch informative video clips.

Key Words
Study vocabulary, and complete a matching word activity.

Quizzes
Test your knowledge.

Slide Show
View images and captions, and prepare a presentation.

Embedded Weblinks
Gain additional information for research.

Try This!
Complete activities and hands-on experiments.

AV² was built to bridge the gap between print and digital. We encourage you to tell us what you like and what you want to see in the future.

Sign up to be an AV² Ambassador at www.av2books.com/ambassador.

30